New Curriculum MATHEMATICS for Schools

Key Stage 1   Book 1

Name _____

Ring the **sets**.

The toyshop

Colour.

a set of red toys

a set of blue toys

a set of green toys

a set of yellow toys

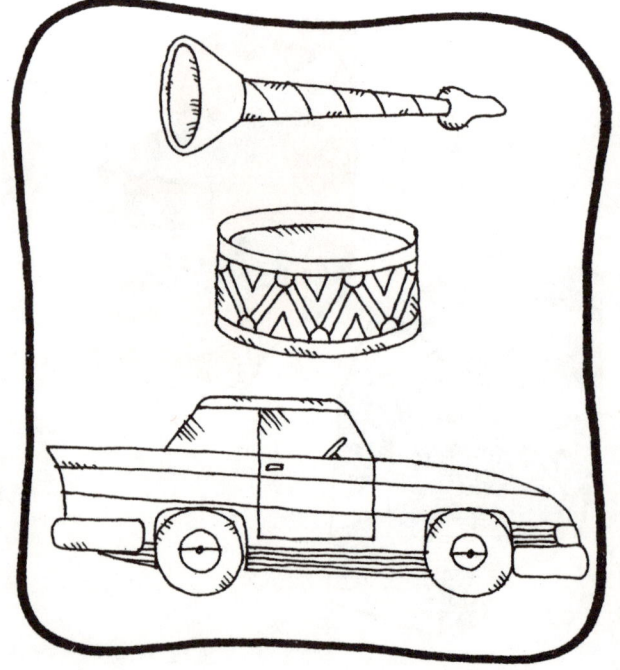

Draw and colour.

The toyshop

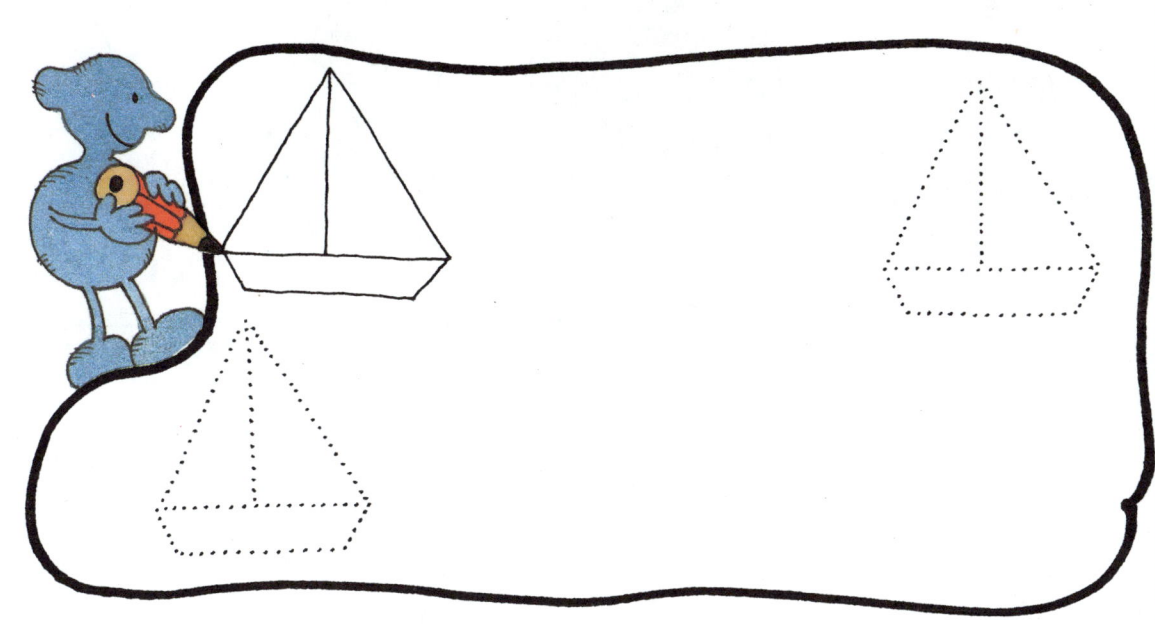

a .... of sailing boats

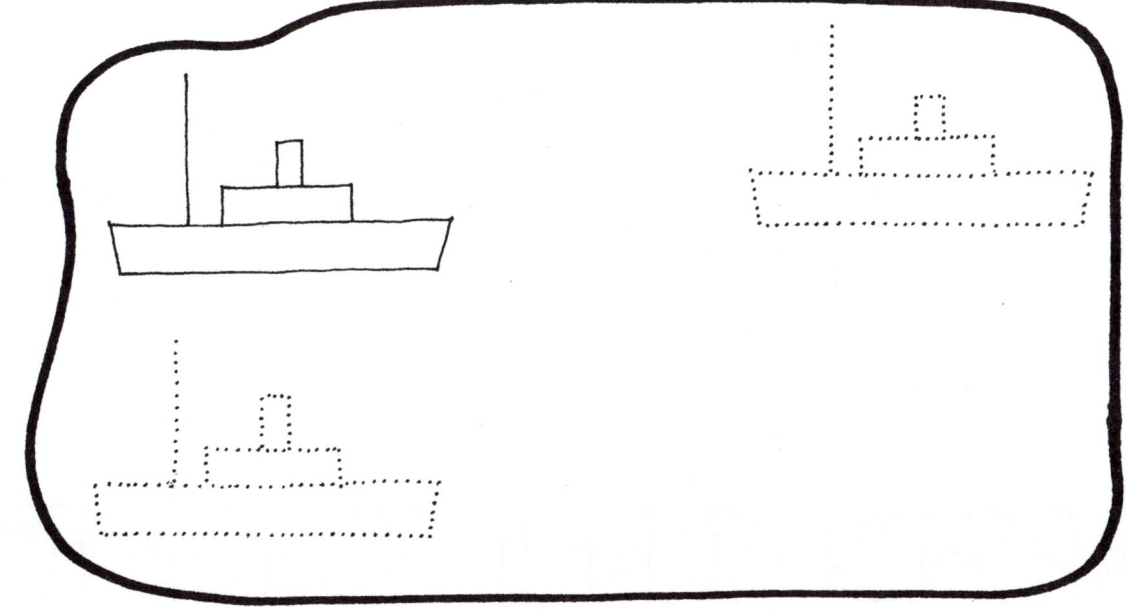

a .... of ships

Carry on the patterns.

Make the pictures the same.

Join. is the same shape as

The supermarket

Ring the sets.

Colour the **cubes** red.

The .... are red.

Colour the **cylinders** green.
Colour the cubes blue.

The .... are green.

Colour the **cuboids** blue.
Colour the cylinders red.

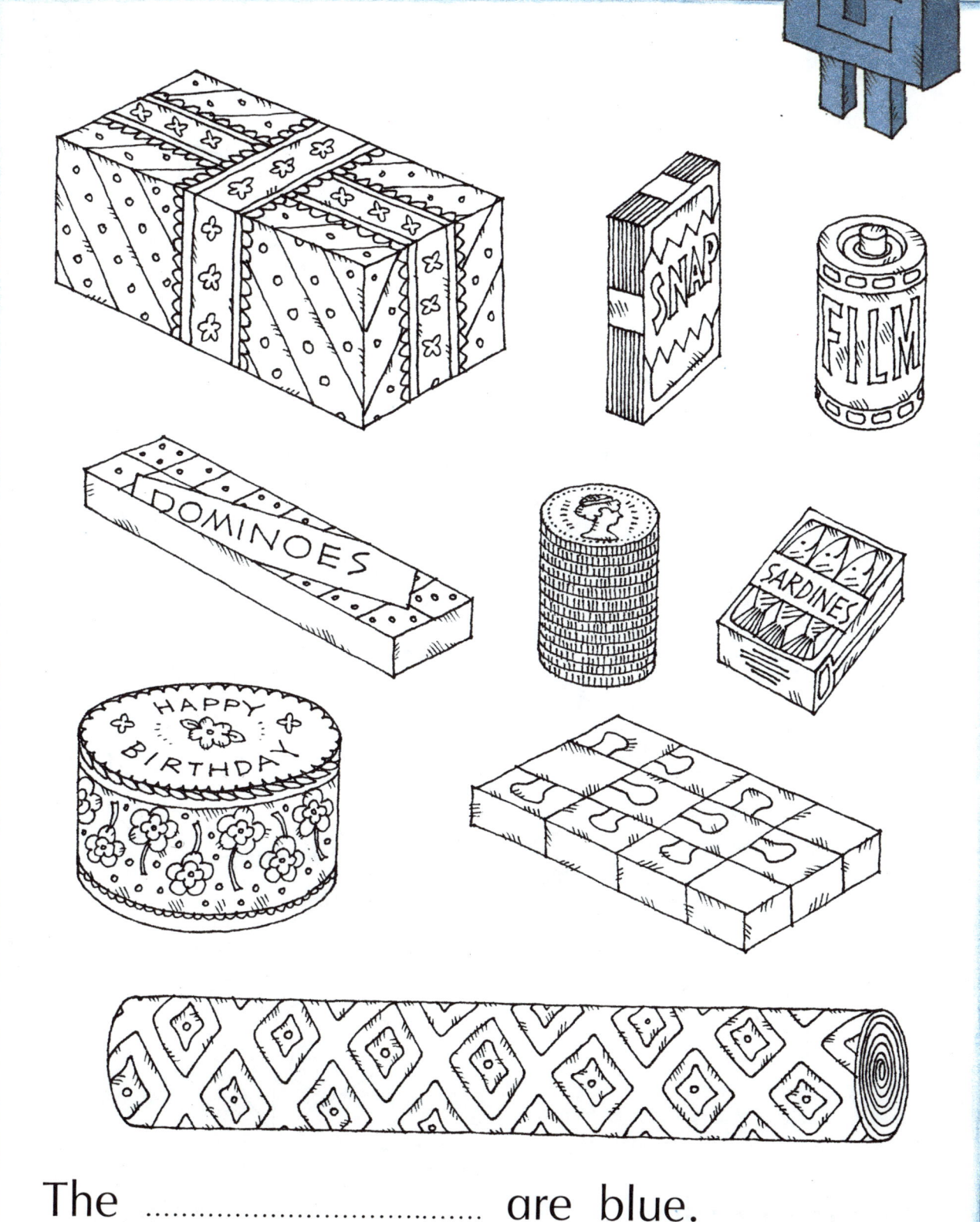

The .... are blue.

Colour the **triangular prisms** yellow.
Colour the cuboids green.

The triangular .... are yellow.

Carry on the pattern.

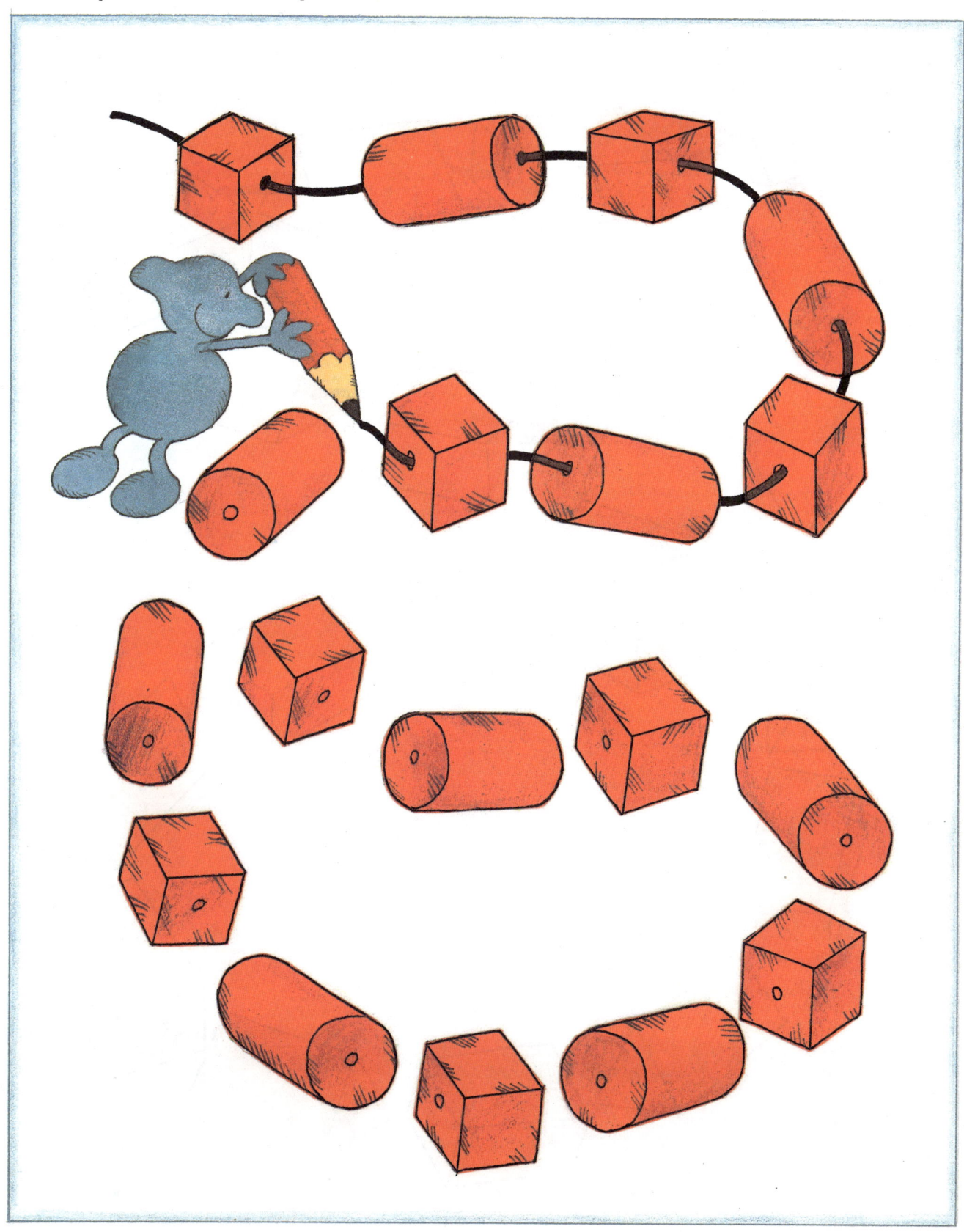

Carry on the pattern.

Join the **large** cubes.

Colour the **small** cubes yellow.

Join the small cylinders.

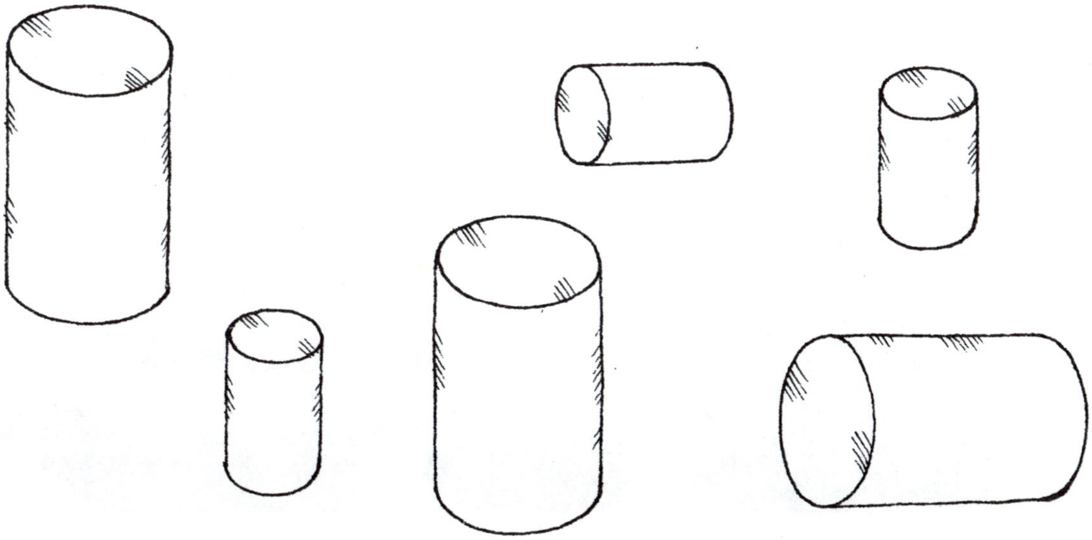

Colour the large cylinders green.

Carry on the patterns.

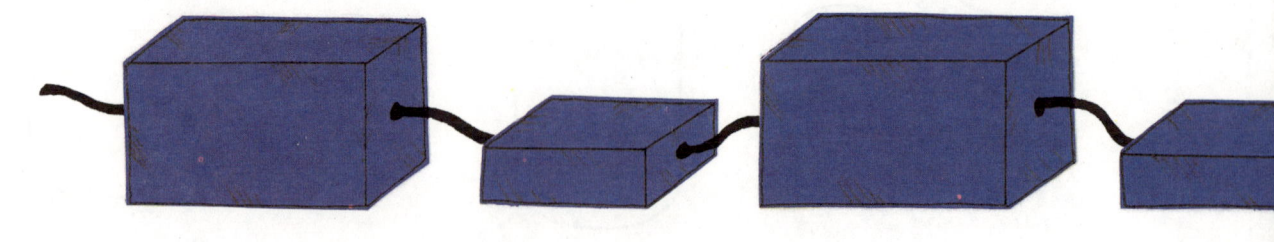

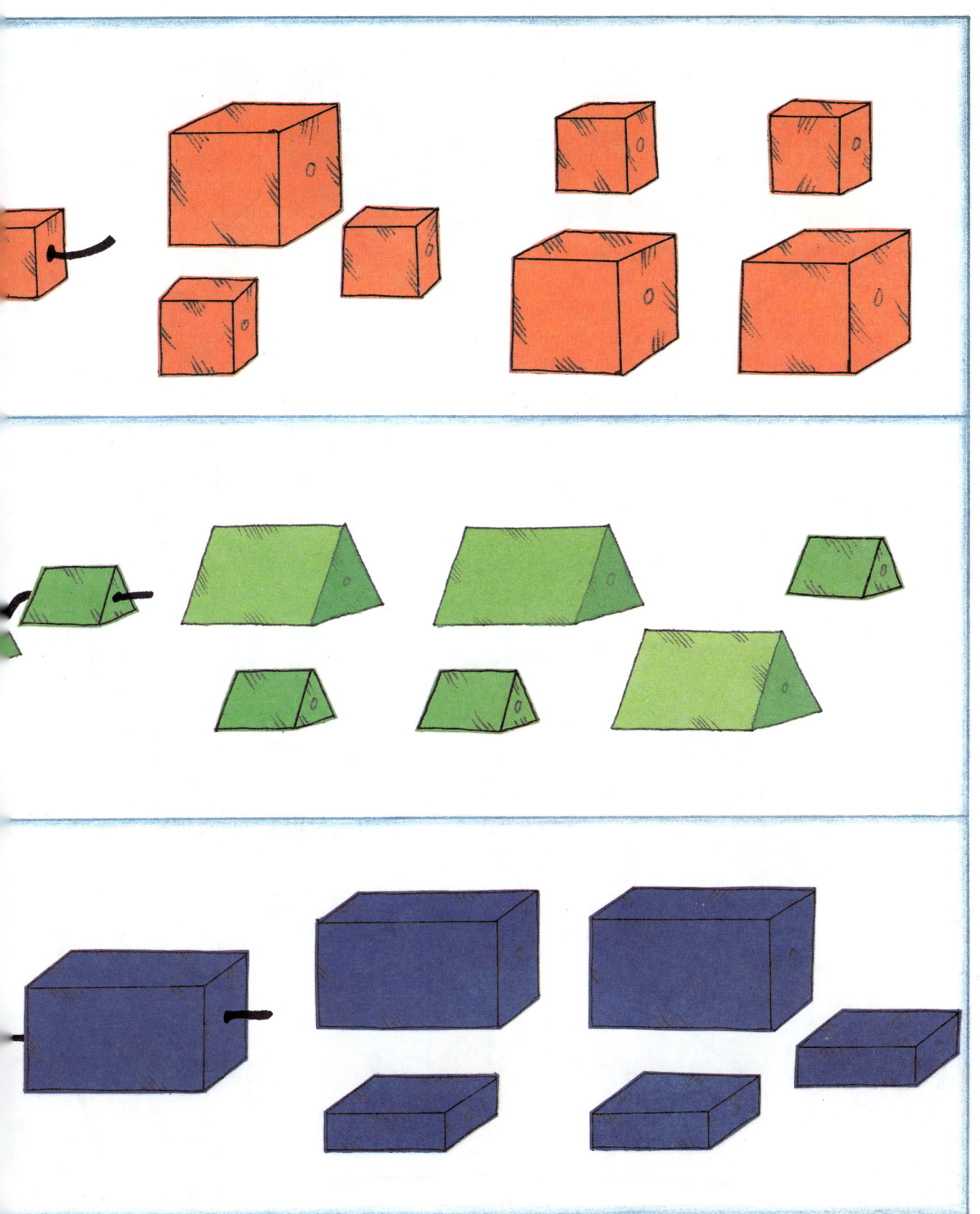

Join the shapes to the words.

Partition the set of shapes.

Partition the set.  At the circus

Partition the set.

 At the circus

Large and small  At the circus

The elephant is large.

The dog is small.

Draw a set of large faces.

Draw a set of small faces.

Draw a set of large balls.

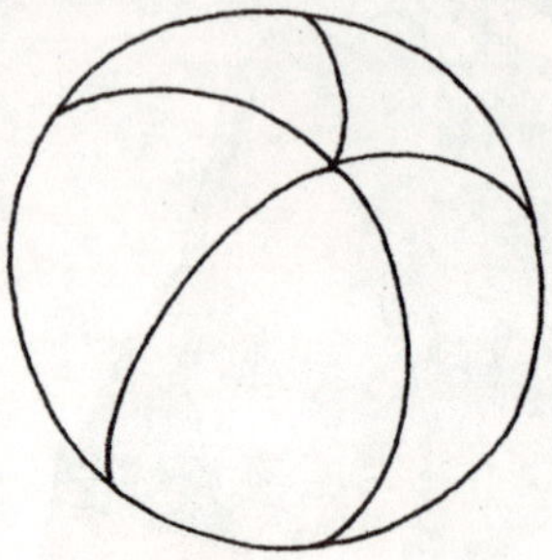

a set of .... red balls

Draw a set of small balls.

a set of .... green balls

Tall and short

The man is **tall**.

The lady is **short**.

Draw a set of tall trees.

.... trees

Draw a set of short trees.

.... trees

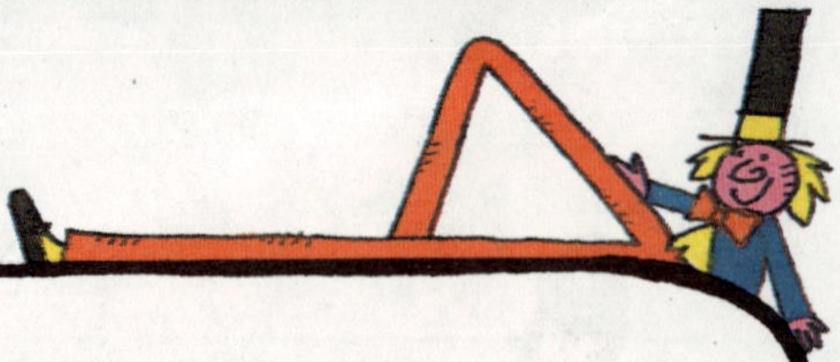

Draw a set of tall people.

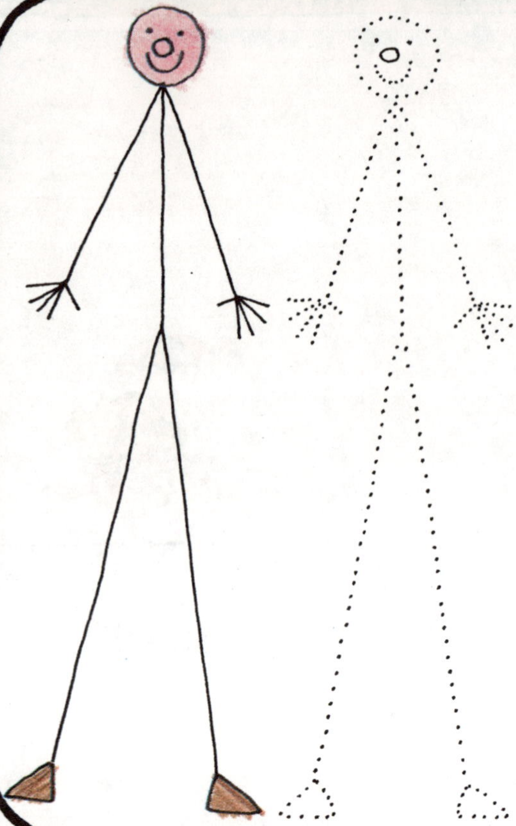

a set of .... people

Draw a set of short people.

a set of .... people

Long and short

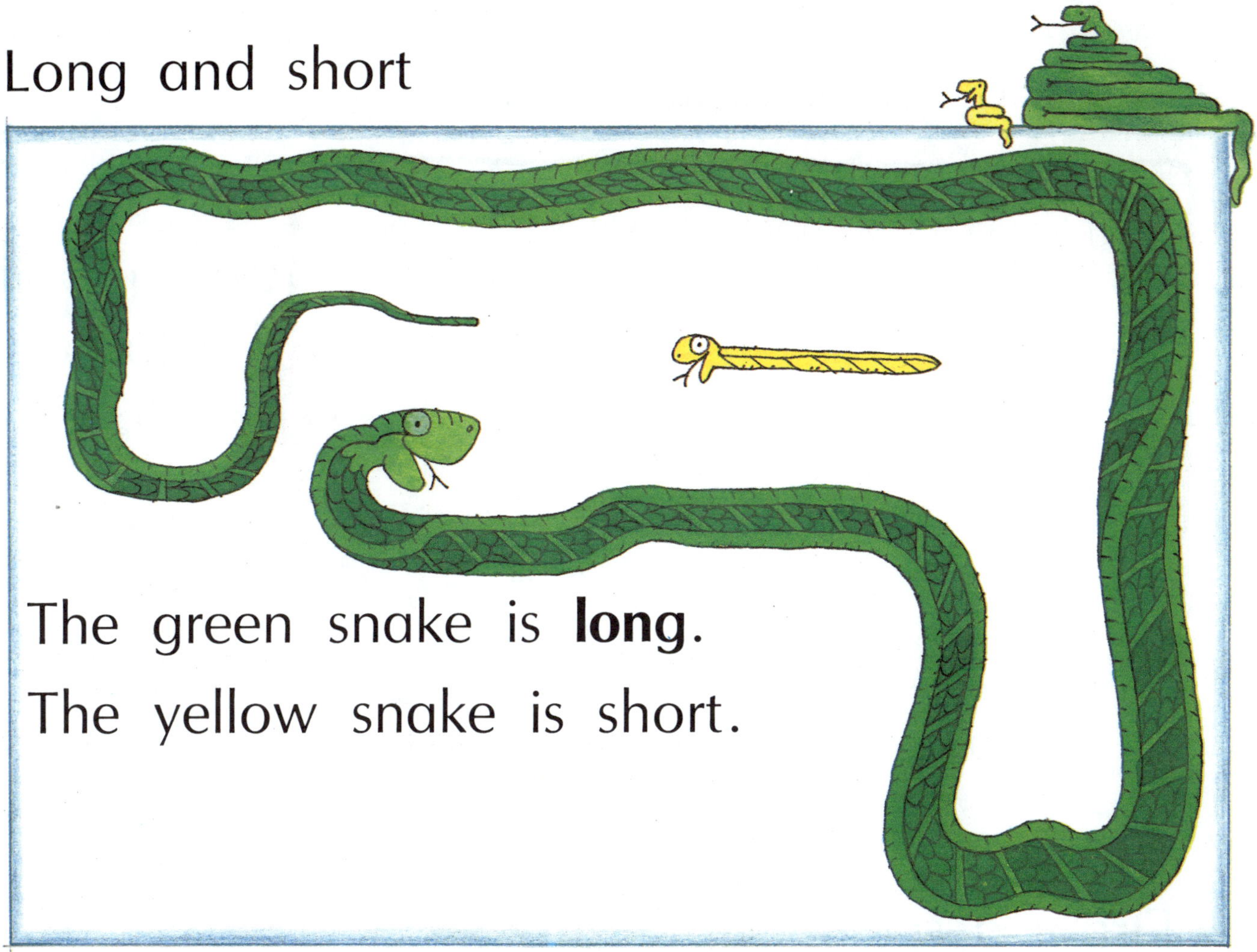

The green snake is **long**.
The yellow snake is short.

Draw a set of long snakes.

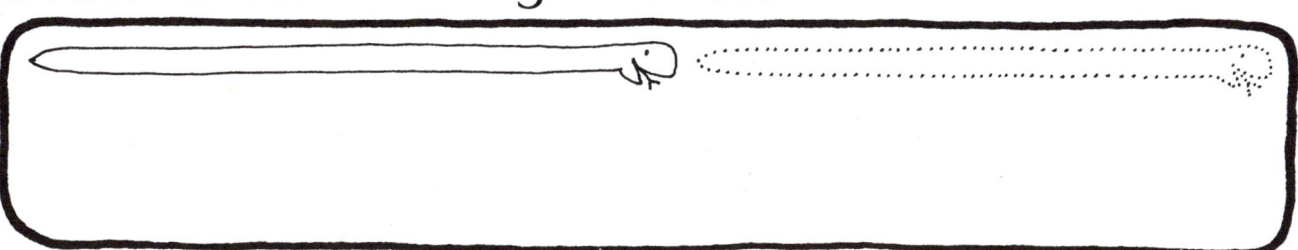

Draw a set of short snakes.

Draw a set of long lorries.

a set of ………………… red lorries

Draw a set of short lorries.

Colour the lorries red.

Colour the short lorries blue.

a set of ………………… blue lorries

At the circus

Carry on the patterns.

'Footprints'

Join.    is the same shape as

Draw a set of **squares**.

a set of
....

Colour the squares.

Partition the set of squares.

Draw a set of **circles**.

a set of ....

Colour the circles.

Partition the set of circles.

Draw a set of **triangles**.

a set of
....

Colour the triangles.

Partition the set of triangles.

Draw a set of **rectangles**.

a set of ....

Colour the rectangles.

Partition the set of rectangles.

Partition the sets of **plane shapes**.

Colour the shapes.

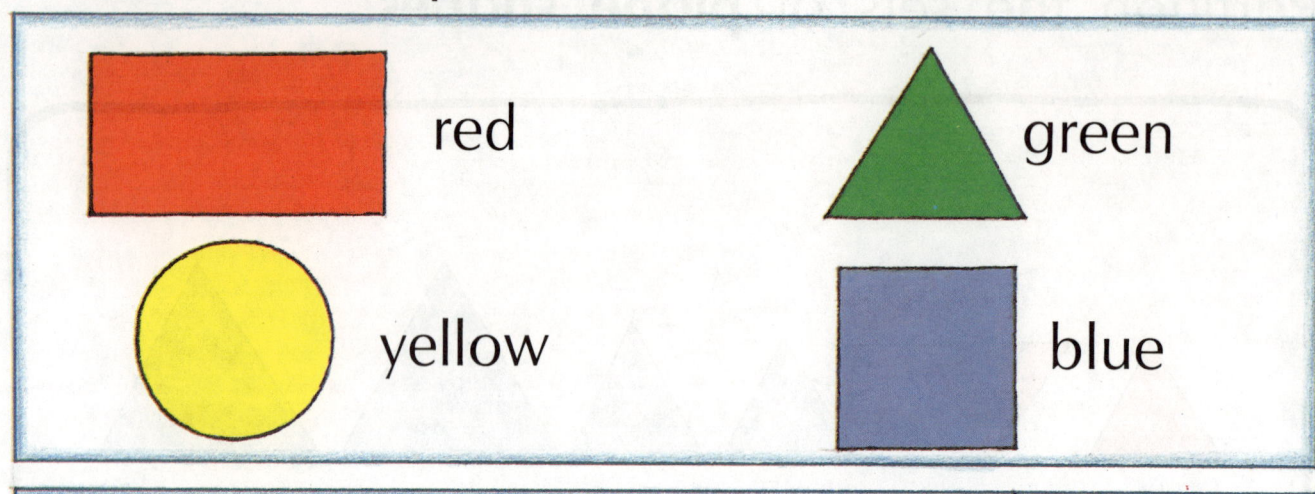

Draw the shapes. Carry on the patterns.

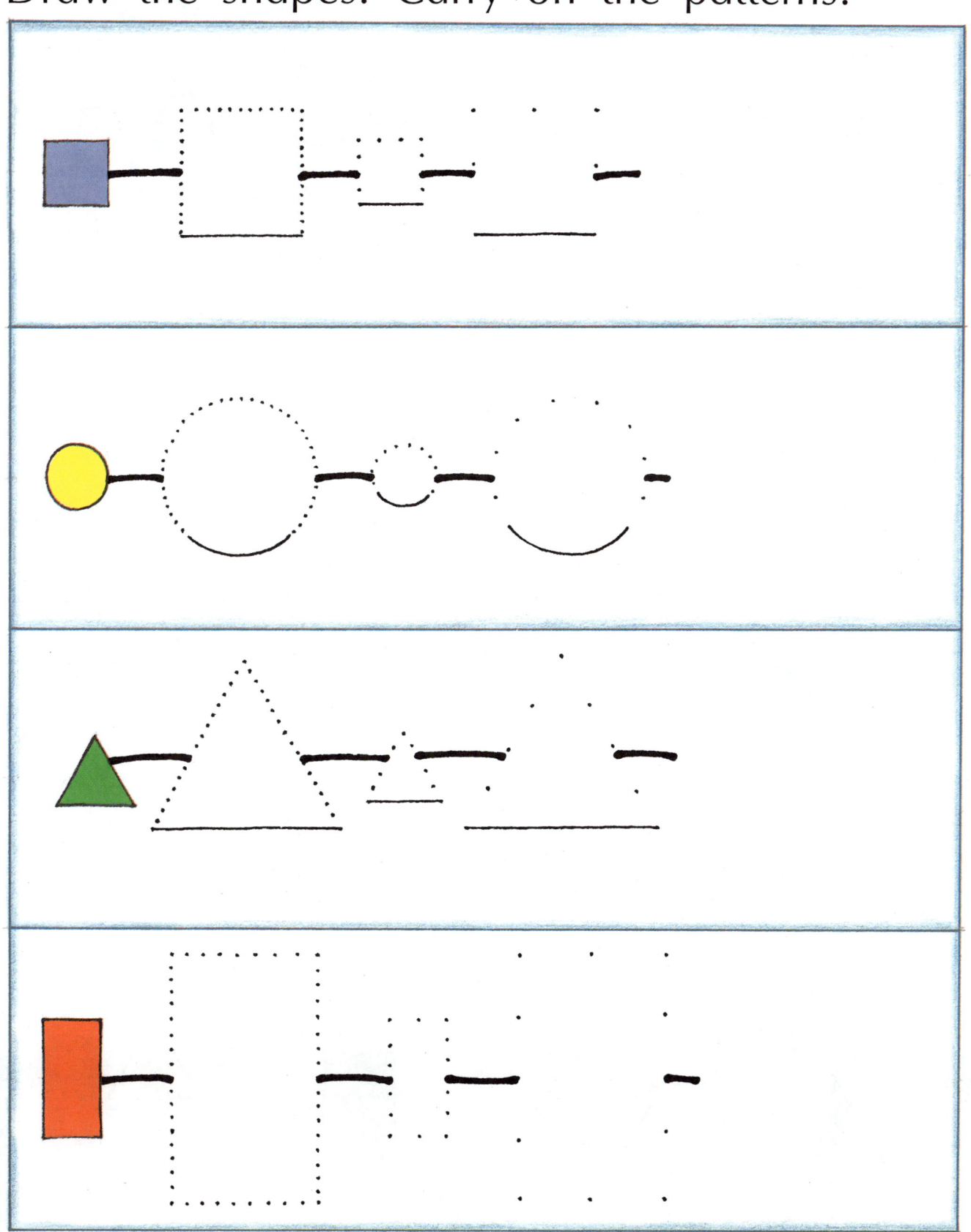

Make colour patterns.

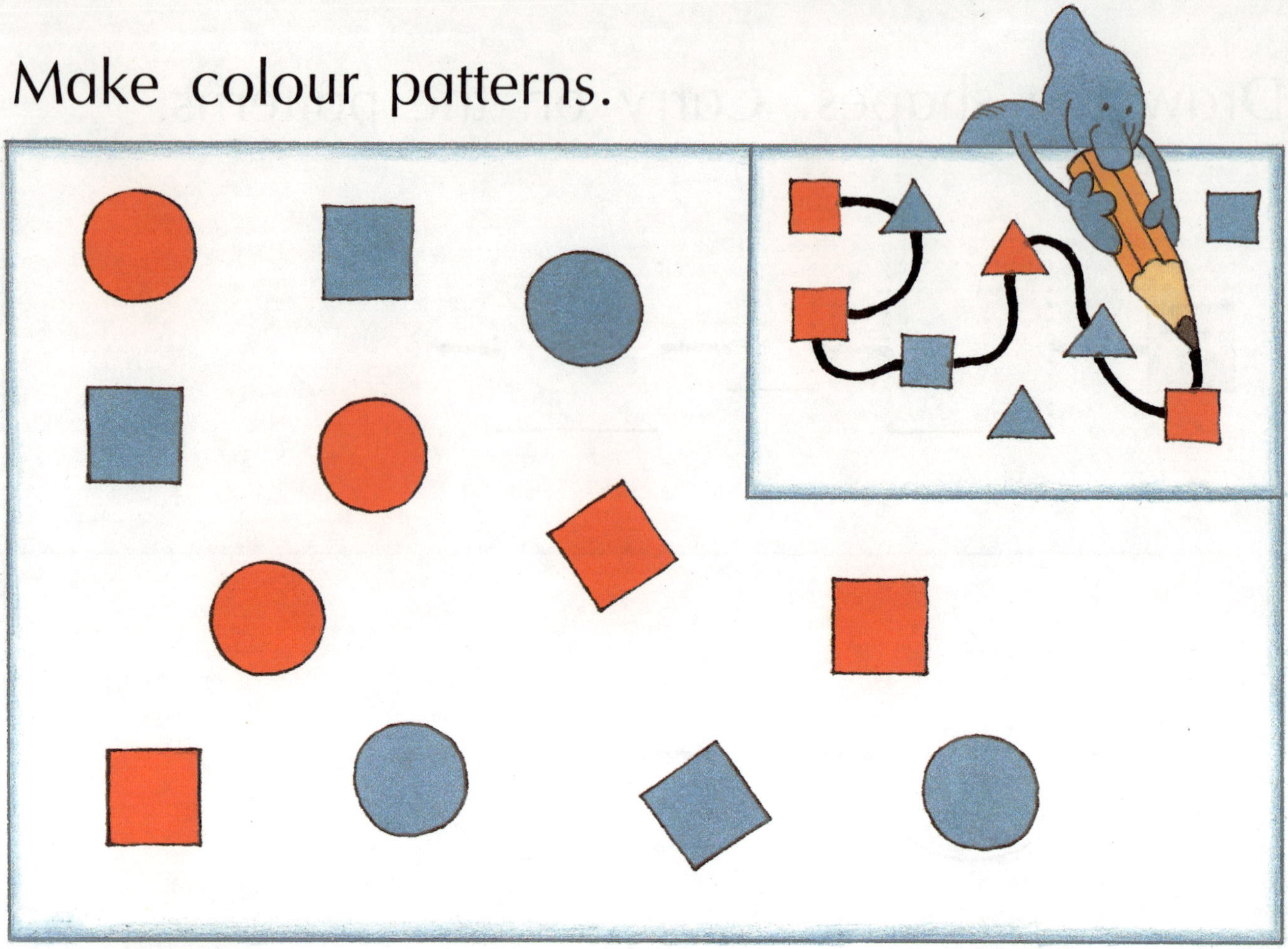

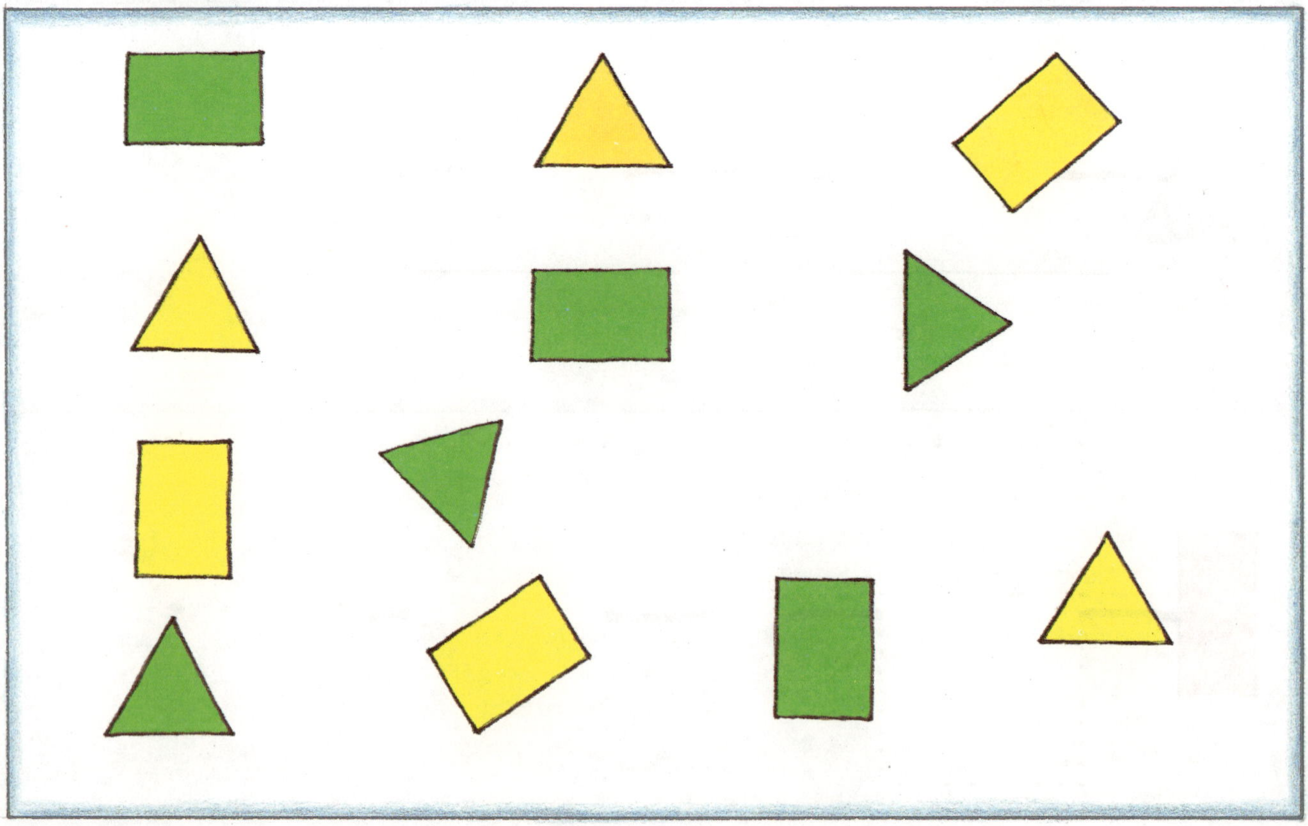

Make plane shape patterns.
Colour the plane shapes.

Join. ← belongs to →

Nursery rhymes

The teddy bears' picnic

Join **one to one**.

Join one to one.

Join. ←belongs to→

The three bears

43

Join each car to a garage.

Has each car a garage? | Yes | No |

Join each car to a space.

Has each car a space? | Yes | No |

Give each child a ball.

Give each child an ice-cream.

The sets **match**.

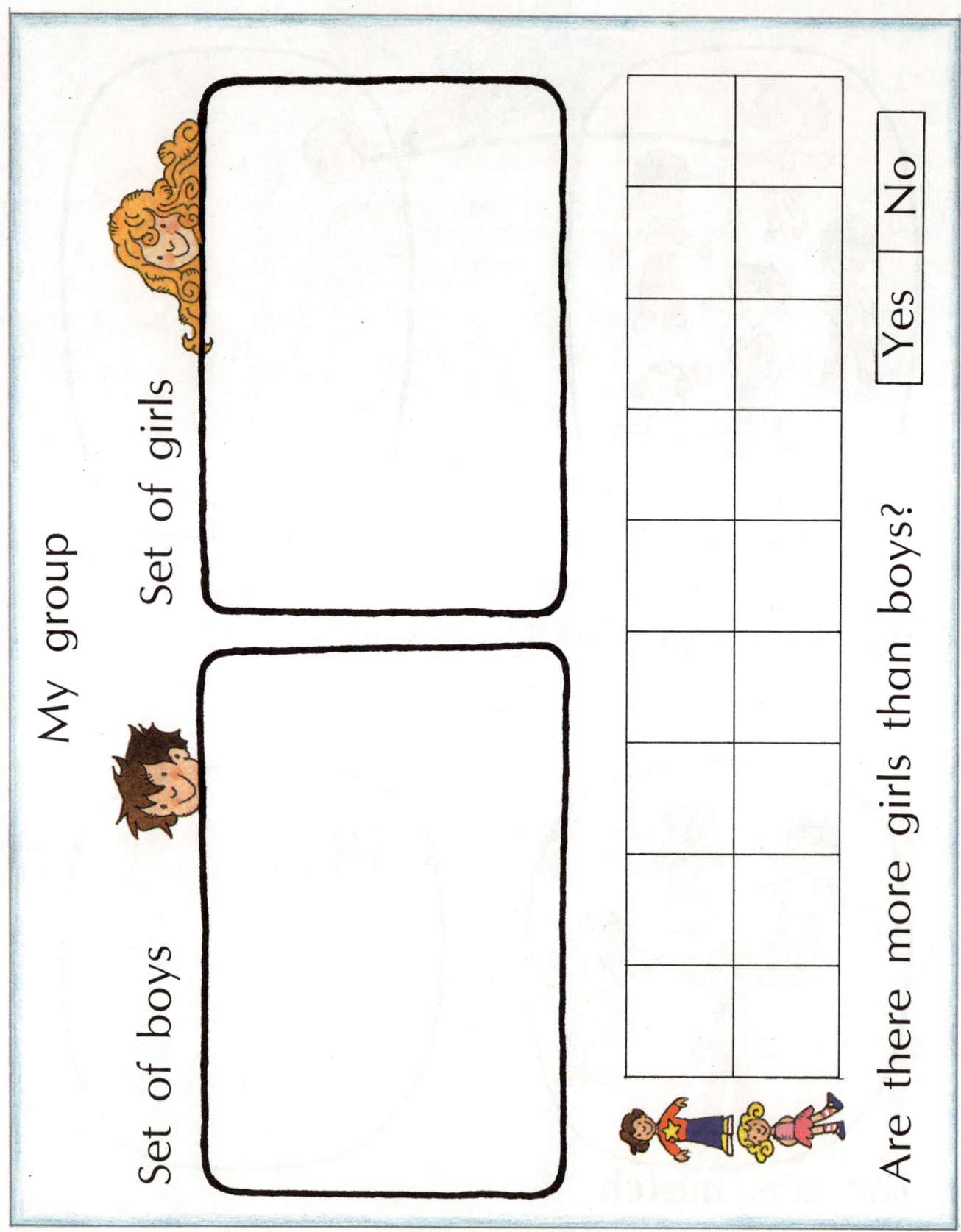

Playtime weather report

Monday	Tuesday	Wednesday	Thursday	Friday

Monday	Tuesday	Wednesday	Thursday	Friday

dry

wet

Were there more dry days than wet? | Yes | No |

New Curriculum MATHEMATICS for Schools

Consultant Editor: Sir Wilfred Cockcroft

Illustrated by John Lobban

Authors: John Marshall (*Coordinator*), John Armstrong, John Page, Linda Parton and Gwyn Price.

© Sir Wilfred Cockcroft, John Marshall, John Armstrong, John Page, Linda Parton and Gwyn Price 1989

Solid shapes introduced in Book 1

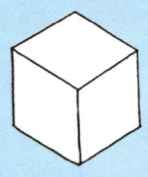 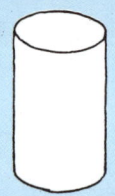  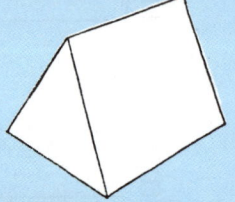

Cube   Cylinder   Cuboid   Triangular prism

Oliver & Boyd, Longman House, Burnt Mill, Harlow, Essex, CM20 2JE

First published 1989

Produced by Longman Group FE Ltd. Printed in Hong Kong

Oliver & Boyd